DISCARD

The Wit and Wisdom of Bishop Fulton J. Sheen

Books by Bill Adler

THE WIT AND WISDOM OF BILLY GRAHAM
THE KENNEDY WIT
THE STEVENSON WIT
THE CHURCHILL WIT
THE WASHINGTON WITS
LETTERS FROM CAMP
KIDS' LETTERS TO THE FBI
KIDS' LETTERS TO PRESIDENT KENNEDY
LETTERS FROM VIETNAM

THE
WIT AND WISDOM
OF
BISHOP
FULTON J. SHEEN

Edited by Bill Adler

PRENTICE-HALL, INC., ENGLEWOOD CLIFFS, N.J.

The Wit and Wisdom of Bishop Fulton J. Sheen
Edited by Bill Adler
© 1968 by Bill Adler
Library of Congress Catalog Card Number: 68-27798
Printed in the United States of America · T
Prentice-Hall International, Inc., London
Prentice-Hall of Australia, Pty. Ltd., Sydney
Prentice-Hall of Canada, Ltd., Toronto
Prentice-Hall of India Private Ltd., New Delhi
Prentice-Hall of Japan, Inc., Tokyo

*I am most grateful
to the staff of
Bill Adler Books, Inc.,
for their assistance
in the preparation of
the manuscript for this book
and especially to
Catherine A. Greene.*

*We are most grateful
to
Bishop Sheen
for his cooperation
in the preparation
of this book.*

CONTENTS

Introduction

On October 26, 1966, Pope Paul VI appointed Fulton J. Sheen Bishop of Rochester, New York. At the age of seventy-one, Bishop Sheen had reached a new pinnacle in his life; the appointment by the Pope was the culmination of almost fifty years of dedicated service to the Catholic Church. And yet his devoted service to America has well equaled his devotion and contributions to his church. He is recognized as one of this nation's—and the world's—best known and loved Catholic priests. His religious appointments are too numerous to list, and his accomplishments as an author, public speaker, educator, and editor are held in the highest esteem by statesmen, educators, and clergymen throughout the world.

However, the uniqueness of his life lies in the fact that his appeal has not been confined to statesmen, clergymen, or Catholics. The universality of his words and the force of his convictions transcend the boundaries of religion and politics. Because of this, he has gained the eyes and ears of an entire nation—a nation whose foundation comprises members of many different religions and ideologies.

Thus, Bishop Sheen speaks a language to all men's

hearts. His words never imply judgment or criticism. To troubled and conflicted people he states that suffering and trials "constitute as much the essence of life as shadows resulting from sunlight." Bishop Sheen's awareness that "shadows" exist in all men's hearts has formed the universality of his appeal.

Fervent as his convictions are concerning each man as an individual—his home, his children, marriage, sex, and his right to private property—equally passionate are his convictions concerning each man in his role as a citizen of this nation. For over thirty years Bishop Sheen has comforted, counseled, and prayed for America through her wars and hardships. He has spoken to the nation over his weekly radio and TV programs, through his newspaper columns, as an editor, and as the author of over sixty books.

A simple listing of all of Bishop Sheen's activities for the past forty years would certainly reveal the extent of his fame, but excluded would be the essence of his appeal. Whether his statements are of a secular or a religious nature, he always presents them in a fresh and invigorating manner. He has raised many questions concerning age-old values, customs, and "formulas" for living. He has questioned the belief that any single and strong virtue can make any man, or country, great. He feels that there must be contrasting virtues: "The possession of one virtue in an eminent degree no more makes a man great than one wing makes a bird. . . . A really great character is not just a brave man, for if a man were brave without being tender, he might very easily become cruel. ... Love for peace alone does not make character, for without the opposite virtue of courage, peacefulness could very easily slip into spineless cowardice."

In the early 1930's, Bishop Sheen was a fervent speaker of the dangers inherent in the Communist system of government. He spoke against Communism's superficial promises and appeals to impoverished nations and peoples. He explained that the Church repudiated this system of government because "she knows you cannot start an earthly paradise by revolution any more than you can make a baby grow by lighting a bomb under its cradle."

Bishop Sheen has objected to America's preoccupation with overpsychoanalyzing and with pampering her children, and he often raised the question: Should parents obey children? He once stated, "Most child psychiatrists today are opposed to spanking. A child psychologist has been defined as one who would never strike a child—except in self-defense."

Bishop Sheen's words are often cushioned with a gentle wit—a wit with which he often makes a point succinctly. In one discussion concerning man's basic drives, he remarked, "Man is not a creature of instincts like an animal. ... Most men do have a hunting instinct, but this does not give them a right to shoot their mother-in-law!"

Covering a wide range of subjects—from juvenile

delinquency to women's fashions—*The Wit and Wisdom of Bishop Fulton J. Sheen* presents the best and most magnetic of his words. A treasury for persons of all religions, its diversity exemplifies Bishop Sheen's conviction that "it is not a unity of religion we plead for . . . but a unity of religious people. . . . We may not be able to meet in the same pew . . . but we can meet on our *knees."*

This collection will be an inspiration for any individual hoping to enrich his private day-to-day life. It will also be a source of inspiration to each of us who takes his responsibility as an American citizen seriously, a responsibility to preserve this nation, whose roots and source of life are religious. Bishop Sheen said in one of his most heartfelt statements: "If you wish to keep your light and heat, you must also keep your sun. If you wish to keep your perfume, you must also keep your flowers. If you wish to keep your forests, you must keep your trees, and if you wish to keep your rights and liberties in education, you must also keep your God. That is the American heritage."

Bill Adler
New York City

❧ LOVE AND MARRIAGE

Sex today is no longer a mystery, inasmuch as it is currently reduced to a pure biological function. Because its mystery, which is a profound love for another person expressed in corporal unity, has been lost, the taboo on sex has disappeared. Sex in a human being is not the same as sex in a pig. Sex in a human is both a function and a communication. As a biological function, it is similar to that of animals. As a communication, it implies another person and is worlds apart.

Eros becomes meaningful when the purpose of the function is to become united with another person. Then it is quasi-divine. When that other person is seen as made in the image and likeness of God, the purpose of sex is the enrichment of personality, by and through another person.

For the beast, love and sex are identical, but not for man. Hence man feels a melancholy and a frustration which is impossible to the beast. If the stomach can eat food and become disgusted with it because it does not nourish the body, so, too, sex can create a melancholy and a sadness when it does not nourish the soul. It may even create a hate of the other person, because having placed the infinite in the other person and not having received it, one is apt to hate that person as a traitor to a pledge; he or she promised something that was not given. But it was something that could never be given. The infinite satisfaction and happiness of love is not to be found on this earth. Such marriages then become like the bumping of two ships together in a narrow channel, or else like two empty glasses that jingle together momentarily, or else as futile in the order of love as two sailors were in the order of economics who supported themselves after being shipwrecked on an island by taking in each other's washing.

Marriage is not a contract based on mood. Nothing permanent will ever be done on the basis of moods. On that basis a farmer could not plant potatoes, because—who knows?—maybe next week he will be in a tomato mood. Houses could never be constructed, nor bridges built, because the builder's mood might change.

A man who marries a woman thinking he will divorce her when his mood changes is also capable of marrying her thinking that he might murder her. No other contract in the world is subject to alteration when the mood changes. No businessman can ever have dealings with another businessman with the proviso that everything will be off if a wrong mood, created by a tweed coat or a mauve necktie, intervenes. Nobody will ever get anything right if everybody's mood is to be equally wrong. The multiplication table does not depend on taste, nor income taxes on our feelings, nor bank trusts on our moods. Then why should marriage, which is the root and ground of all human institutions, even the State, be based on moods?

It is not true that human relations are matters of instinct and in particular of the sex instinct. Man is not a creature of instincts like an animal. Since he is a rational creature, his instincts are to be directed reasonably. Most men have a hunting instinct, but this does not give them a right to shoot their mothers-in-law. There are times, too, when an instinct has to be suppressed; a husband must often suppress an instinct for his wife's sake, and the wife must suppress an instinct for her husband's sake.

Nor is it any truer to say that marriage is based on sex adjustment than that education is based on teacher-student adjustment. Marriage is based on love, not sex, sex being one of the means God has instituted for the deepening of love between husband and wife. Sex is biological and has its definite zones of satisfaction; under certain circumstances, love includes all of these, but it is directed to the *totality* of the person loved—his or her mind, body, soul. To make marriage a matter of sex adjustment is to reduce human beings to the level of jackals and the ethics of the home to the practices of a barnyard. Animals feel, but man loves.

Why is it that lovers always speak of "our love" and understand it as something more than the addition of the love of each? They feel themselves as pulled together by some bond outside of them, so that instead of two in love there seem to be three. There is the beloved, the lover, and love. What is this but a reflection of the Triune God, where Lover, Beloved, and God are one?

Why is it that everything becomes part of their love? Moon and stars, flowers and the birds, evening skies, waterfalls, and the fresh breath of springtime all seem to be ministers to their love. This can only be because love is already in them, put there as they fell from the hand of Uncreated Love. Lovers have better vision than others, and that is why they can see in things the love God put there.

To be the victim of an unhappy marriage does not necessarily mean one is deprived of happiness. There are levels of happiness. One is the level of the flesh, another the level of the mind, another the level of the Divine. The law running through the universe is that no one ever mounts to a higher love without dying to a lower one. Love either mounts it or it dies. When the roadway of the flesh is blocked, the highway of the spirit can be opened. What is true in marriage is also true in the spiritual life. Souls dedicated to God often have the "dark night of the soul" as the married have the "dark night of the body." In both cases the acceptance of trials and sacrifice is the condition of finding richer areas of love.

Suffering is bearable if there is someone we love. No human being is free to decide whether he will go through life without suffering and trial. These constitute as much the essence of life as shadows resulting from sunlight. Our choice is only to decide how we will react to them. Some trials in marriage are of such a magnitude that no human remedy can help; it is then that one must turn to God and the fullness of His love.

Beauty in a woman and strength in a man are two of the most evident spurs to love. Physical beauty and vitality increase vigor in each other, but it is to be noticed that beauty in a woman and strength in a man are given by God to serve the purposes of allurement. They come at that age of life when men and women are urged to marry one another. They are not permanent possessions. They are something like the frosting on a cake, or like the electric starter of an automobile motor. If love were based only on the fact that she is a model and he is a fullback on a football team, marriage would never endure. But just as the frosting on the cake leads to the cake itself, so too do these allurements pass on to greater treasures.

Once, on congratulating a wife who had a very handsome husband, we heard her reply, "I no longer notice that he is handsome; I notice now that he has greater qualities."

Each instinct and passion of man is amoral; it is only the abuse of these passions that makes them wrong. There is nothing wrong about hunger, but there is something wrong about gluttony; there is no sin in thirst, but there is a sin in drunkenness; there is nothing wrong with a man who seeks economic security, but there is something wrong with a man who is avaricious; there is nothing to be despised in knowledge, but there is something to be condemned in pride; there is nothing wrong with the flesh, but there is something wrong in the abuse of the flesh. Just as dirt is matter in the wrong place, so sin is flesh in the wrong place. Dirt is all right on a road, but it is all wrong on a table. Sex has its place in that area of life designed for its fruition, but the misuse of it outside of that natural and supernatural bond is wrong.

The Victorians wrote about love as if sex were never involved. Even the body was clothed with yards and yards of bottle green, carrot red, brown and dirty ocher; human beings reached a point where they had as many coats as onions. Men wore beards which covered their faces and their necks. It was an era in which many wished to be free from all mention of sex, unless it was sin in another. A woman once told Dr. Johnson when he was preparing his dictionary, "I am so glad there are no impure words in your dictionary." Dr. Johnson answered, "How did you know? Did you look for them?"

. . . though the love of man differs from an animal, the love that is in the soul is related to a body. Nothing that exists in the mind ever came, at least in its humble beginings, to be a part of knowledge except through the senses. Even the purest and sublimest loves of the soul cannot express themselves except in symbols derived in part from the body. Furthermore, the greatest of all thinkers, Thomas Aquinas, said that there is no moment in which the body and soul are in closer relation and in which there is a greater repercussion of one on the other than in the union of husband and wife.

. . . inasmuch as love involves both body and soul, it follows that there are two possible kinds of error. One is the Victorian error, which emphasized the soul in love without the body; the other is the Freudian error, which emphasized the body without the soul. Within a century the world has passed from one extreme, in which sex was a subject nobody could talk about, to our present period, where people can talk about nothing else.

Love is very much like sunlight, which in prehistoric time bathed the trees of the forest. Later on, they sank into the earth and finally were dug up as coal. When the coal burns, it returns again the debt of light and heat which it took from the sun. So the human heart receives its capacity and its desire for love from God as the trees receive sunlight; later on, in union with another heart, love burns and returns again to God the the love that came from Him.

The secret of a happy nation and peaceful hearts is the realization that, in a proposal and in love, every man and woman promise one another something that only God can give. Human love seems in its beginning to promise infinite felicity; but only Perfect Love can do this. To repose in the symbol and to forget the reality is to be deceived. But once one starts with the truth that the human heart is love on pilgrimage, then two hearts can combine to achieve Perfect Love, which is outside both. Love is like bread; man hungers for it and needs it, but not by bread alone doth man live; only a Heavenly Bread can satisfy the cravings of the heart. The other partner is merely a messenger but not the message; he, or she, is a John the Baptist announcing a Messiah of Perfect Love. Hence the ecstasies of the human heart are to be taken as symbols, and sacraments, and telltales, of the Divine. As lovers clasp each other in the embrace of love, the greatest wisdom and happiness is in whispering to one another: "If the human heart can so thrill us, then what must be the great Heart of God!"

If life is to be happy, there must be a community of interest that extends beyond the physical. This is not easy to establish because men most often talk about things, and women most often talk about persons. If there is wanting a deep sense of mutualness, the husband may come home one night saying, "Today I sold a thousand refrigerators," to which the wife may answer, "How do you want your eggs?" To cement harmony, there must be an interest in one another; as they are two in one flesh, so they must be two in one heart and mind. A marriage where there is no common interest makes husband and wife like two birds trying to get together through a windowpane that separates them.

In true married love it is not so much that two hearts walk side by side through life. Rather the two hearts become one heart. That is why death is not the separation of two hearts, but rather the tearing apart of one heart. It is this that makes the bitterness of grief. . . .

The curve of love was meant to be an ascension, for love is a messenger. A messenger brings an envelope or a package which is visible and material; but inside the envelope is something invisible and immaterial. Life is like that, and love is like that. A handshake is a messenger. It is much more than the clasping of two hands, for if we clasp our own hands, we would never say that it was a handshake. The material element, or that which is seen, is the grasping of the hand; the invisible element is the communication of welcome and friendship. . . .

Love was meant to be also a sign, a symbol, a messenger, a telltale of the Divine. The material element in it is the fact that all love comes from God. Love is a messenger from God saying that every human affection and every ecstasy of love is a spark from the great flame of love which is God.

True love is born of a need and a sympathy. The need is a result of our creatureliness, which, being imperfect, seeks a fulfillment. The eye needs light; the ear needs harmony; the stomach needs food; and the heart needs love. It is not good for man to be alone. Sympathy, on the other hand, is born of our Godlikeness; created by God Whose Goodness seeks to diffuse Itself, we too have a summons to forget self, a mandate to serve others, a commandment to love neighbor as self. The thirst for more is the mark of man, the creature; the pouring out of refreshment for others is the mark of God. To want to be more than we are is earthly; to want to be less than we are by spending ourselves on others is heavenly.

❦ FREEDOM IN AMERICA

What is the American heritage that we have to defend through education? The American heritage, I think, is respect for human rights and liberties. That brings up this next question: Where do we get our rights and liberties which we have to defend? They have a source. Where do I get the right of free speech? Where does the Board of Regents get the right to educate? Where do you get freedom of conscience, freedom of religion? Do you get them from the State of New York? If you got them from the State of New York, the State of New York could take them away. Do you get your rights and liberties from the Federal Government in Washington? If you got your rights and liberties from the Federal Government in Washington, the Federal Government in Washington could take them away.

Our Founding Fathers had to face this question, and it was one of the very first that they answered. . . . They sought for some basis and ground of human rights and liberties, and they found it and set it down in the second paragraph of the Declaration of Independence: It is a self-evident principle that the Creator—the *Creator*—has endowed man with certain inalienable rights. They cannot be taken away. And among them is the right to life, liberty, and the pursuit of happiness.

Some time ago I was invited to be on the committee of a rather well known group in the United States. Among other reasons, I declined because that same group sponsored a much publicized attack on religion by a rather well-known scientist.

An appeal was made to my broad-mindedness. "After all, you would not be intolerant, would you?"

I asked this particular official if he had a child. Admitting he had, I said: "Suppose your child was taken seriously ill. Five doctors were called in and all admitted it was a dangerous streptococcus infection. But three of them said to you: "We know that there are rather intolerant specialists who say that a streptococcus infection is dangerous, but after all, this is healthy and what is unhealthy is purely relative. Personally we think that you should be broad-minded about this germ, and allows us to develop it, for we seem to have a particularly good culture in your child."

I then asked him: "What would you say to those doctors?" He said: "I would order them out, for the life of my child is worth more than the life of a germ."

But I said: "Aren't you a bit intolerant? In any case, if you consider the life of the soul more than the body, and the preservation of inalienable rights as a gift of God more precious than the feelings of an antireligious scientist, why is it wrong for me to refuse to be a member of a committee which sponsors lectures destructive of democracy and the country I love? If you are intolerant to a streptococcus germ which destroys a body, why should I not be intolerant about an evil which destroys the nation?"

❖❖❖❖❖❖❖❖❖❖❖❖❖❖❖❖❖❖❖❖❖❖❖❖

If you wish to keep your light and heat, you must also keep your sun. If you wish to keep your perfume, you must also keep your flowers. If you wish to keep your forests, you must keep your trees, and if you wish to keep your rights and liberties in education, you must also keep your God. That is the American heritage.

Democracy cannot survive where there is such uniformity that everyone wears exactly the same intellectual uniform or point of view. Democracy implies diversity of outlook, a variety of points of view on politics, economics, and world affairs. Hence the educational ideal is not uniformity, but unity, for unity allows diversity of points of view regarding the good means to a good end. Hence those who are making the greatest contribution to the unity of America are private schools, Jewish schools, and the religious schools both Protestant and Catholic, which do not have to insist on education as a means of making money and which are free to promote purer knowledge and which are more immune to standardized opinion.

✦✦✦

In 1954, at the annual convention of the National Catholic Education Association, Bishop Sheen spoke on "Education in America." He spoke fervently about the troubled times and stated:

Because our times are apocalyptic, because man has reached a stage where with four hundred cobalt bombs it would be possible to destroy all life upon the face of the earth, because thirty-seven out of one hundred people in the world today are cut by Communist sickles and beaten by Communist hammers, because the modern exile of God has ended in tyrannization of man, it follows that we must approach the problems of education very differently from the way we have approached them in the past. Since we are loyal Americans, since our country under Providence is destined to be a secondary cause for the preservation of the liberties of the world, it behooves us as Catholic educators to concentrate on three great tasks:

1. To save our civilization from authoritarianism.
2. To preserve it from straitjacket uniformity.
3. To keep the foundations of our rights and liberty.

✦✦✦

Now to consider the argument of the Communists that religion makes man passive.

There is probably no perversion of the truth greater than this statement of Communism. It is the contrary that is true. Religion is essentially *dynamic*. The Church, it is true, does preach resignation to our lot, but this does not mean passivity. Rather it is resignation oriented toward action. Resignation means accepting our lot while awaiting better things which are to be attained, not by revolution, but by intelligent action. Is not that the attitude of a mother toward her babe? She is resigned to its infancy, but that does not mean she refuses to nurse it and educate it until it grows into adolescence and maturity. The farmer who sows his seed resigns himself to the fact that it must grow by a slow, mysterious process, for not even by taking thought can he add to its stature one cubit. But such resignation does not mean he does not cultivate his crop, or does not pull up the weeds or welcome the embrace of the sun and rain. In like manner, when the Church speaks of Christian resignation, she means we must effectively work for social amelioration as the farmer with his seed; that is, we must realize that every reform must proceed from a true consideration of the *nature* of the thing to be reformed. She repudiates the Communist system, for she knows that you cannot start an earthly economic paradise by revolution any more than you can make a baby grow by lighting a bomb under its cradle.

If it be objected that the Christian believes in violence for the Kingdom of Heaven "suffereth violence," it must be answered that the violence of the Christians is poles apart from Communistic violence. The Communist believes in violence against his neighbor; the Christian believes in violence against himself—that is, against his pride, his selfishness, his sinfulness, his hate, in a word, against those lower passions which would make him a Communist.

All ideologies of Fascism, Nazism, and Communism seek to confine the purpose of man within the phenomenal limits of blood or a party. By forcing man to surrender to their final authority, they cut man off absolutely from the very ends to which he had already become indifferent through irreligion. The world-man as a result has thrown dust in his own eyes and then had his eyes plucked out so that he no longer can find the gate which leads back home. He was told religion was an opium and eternal purpose only theological folklore and that if he dispossessed himself of his obligations and worries, he could make a paradise of this world. Foolishly man did this, but instead of finding his material life enriched, he discovers that it becomes more precarious each day, without the consolations of hoping for anything beyond the grave of a tomorrow. Having lost the purpose of life he now has left only purposes which are so many loose ends he can never piece together.

There is no way to stop this betrayal of liberty than by Christianity preaching the purpose of man; namely, the social, economic, and political unfolding of his personality in this world and his spiritual efflorescence in the next.

Those who have their finger on the pulse of contemporary civilization have probably noted that there are two contradictory charges against religion today: the first is that religion is not political enough; the other is that religion is too political.

... these two contradictory charges have been leveled against the person of Christ in His body the Church. His Church is accused of being not political enough when it condemns Nazism and Fascism; it is accused of being too political when it condemns Communism. It is said to be too unpolitical when it does not condemn a political regime which some other political systems dislike but which allows religious freedom; it is said to be too political or Fascist when it condemns a political regime which completely suppresses all religion. Would to heaven that man were forced to give definitions of words. Is the Church Fascist? If Fascism means, as it does, the supremacy of the state or nation over the individual, with consequent suppression of rights or liberties, then the Church is anti-Fascist, as the encyclical against Fascism so well proves. If by Fascism is meant anti-Communism and dislike of a system which suppresses the liberties, then the Church is Fascist, but so is every American who loves the democratic way of life. In truth, the proper way to handle this confusion of tongues is to speak of all forms of totalitarianism as Fascism. This divides them into black, brown, and red. Hence we ought to speak of Communism from this time on as Red Fascism. There is an essential resemblance between Nazism and Communism. Fascism is the subordination of the person to the State, Nazism to the race, and Communism to the classes. The only difference between these three forms of totalitarianism is the difference between burglary, larceny, and stealing.

A cow has no rights. Neither has a pig. No animal has rights except by association with a human. We alone have rights, and that is because we have transcendental ends, because we have an immortal soul and because this soul was created by God. Just as soon as education, civilization, and so-called culture alienate themselves from this divine basis of human rights and liberties, there is tyranny.

The right to property flows directly from my personality, and the more intimately things are associated with my person, the more personal is my right to them; the more they receive the impress of my rational nature, the more they are my own. That is why writings, which are the immediate creation of a mind, and why children, which are the immediate products of a body, are so very much man's own. That is why the State will protect an author by copyright laws, and why the State recognizes that the right of education belongs to the parents rather than to the State itself. Man's right to have, then, follows from his right to be himself or live his own life.

... private property is the economic guarantee of human freedom. *Economic* guarantee, for the *spiritual* guarantee of freedom is the fact that each man has a soul he can call his own. But there must be some *external* sign of that inner freedom—that is, something he can call his own on the *outside* because he calls his soul his own on the inside. Freedom means responsibility for one's acts, but how can this interior mastery of one's acts be better guaranteed than by the ownership of something external over which he can exercise control?

Just as an artist is most free to express his spiritual ideas when he owns the canvas, the brush, and the paints, so man knows he is responsible when he exercises responsibility. Because the owner of shares of stock admits no responsibility to his ownership, he ignores the rights of workers, and because the worker *has* no responsibility, he may stop work even when the nation needs it. Hence private property is the external guarantee of human freedom. That is why slaves were deemed not to be free, because they had no property. *They were property.* Morality says: Because I *am,* I may *have;* to *have* is the legitimate extension of my *being.* Property and freedom are one and the same problem.

Power follows property, and they who own things to a great extent own persons. That is why in Russia, since all the productive property is in the hands of a few selfish opportunists, the citizens may go to the polls, but they may never exercise their freedom. So, too, under a highly capitalistic system, the laborers may vote for the president of their country, but they have nothing to say about the industry where they work. Once you concentrate property in the hands of the few, you create slaves; when you decentralize it, you restore liberty. The objection of the Church to slavery is not that the slaves are poor. Slaves need not all be poor. Some are very rich in Russia, as some were very rich in Rome and comfortable on the southern plantations. No! The Catholic approach is quite different. It starts with the fact that no material thing, not even the whole world, shall be allowed to interfere with the right of a person to attain his ultimate end by the exercise of his free will. Why is the Church opposed to low wages? Because low wages make it impossible to have an automobile and a 16-tube radio and an electric kitchen? No! But because unless he has the necessities of a decent, normal, comfortable existence, he is not independent enough to save his soul.

Property has a double aspect: individual and social; the *right* to property is *personal,* but the use or the *function* of property is *social*. It is not quite right to think of property as being divided only into "mine" and "thine." The Church reminds us that there is also such a thing as "our property," because in certain circumstances the "right of others" weighs upon my right; in case of extreme misery it may become an "individual right." For example, the right to life is higher than the right to property; hence, if a rich man refuses bread to a man dying of starvation, and he had no other way of obtaining bread, the dying man has a right to take what is necessary to preserve his life, and this would not be stealing. He could not do so if the right to property were absolute and unconditioned by its use. Normally, the "social function" of property, however, is determined by those who have the care of society.

How sound and fundamental is this distinction between right and use can be seen by reducing it to the concrete. For example, you may own as private property the carpets on your floor, but a city ordinance forbids you to shake them out your apartment windows, because your right to property is *socially conditioned*— that is, by the use you make of it in relationship to your fellow man. You may have a right to your own automobile as private property, but you may not use it to drive on sidewalks. You may own a wine cellar, but you may not use it to put yourself and your neighbors in a state of intoxication; you may own a piece of property, but you may not build a bar upon it directly adjoining a school. The question then of how one uses one's possessions is not inseparable and unrelated to one's right to them. The right to own may be personal, but the right is to some extent conditioned by the use. The basic idea is that we may not so exercise our rights as to injure or interfere with the common good, and if we be Christians, we must always make use of our rights in such a way as to aid our brother in Christ in coming to his full spiritual stature as a member of the Mystical Body of Christ.

Freedom does not mean the right to do whatever we please, but rather to do whatever we ought. Certainly we can do whatever we please: we can drop bags of water out of office windows; we can pull spikes out of railroad ties; we can break school windows; but *ought* we? The right to do whatever we *please* reduces freedom to a physical power and forgets that freedom is a moral power. Ought-ness implies law, order, purpose, goals, and finality. We are free within the law and not outside it. We are free to drive our cars in traffic if we obey traffic laws; we are free to draw triangles if we obey the nature of a triangle and give it three sides, not, in a stroke of broad-mindedness, four. Self-expression can be wrong then as well as right. A boiler is self-expressive when it exceeds the pressure limit imposed on it by its maker; a train is self-expressive when it jumps the tracks and makes its own way. When self-expression is identified with irrational surrender to lower instincts, it ends by making the person a slave to those passions. Self-denial is not a renunciation of freedom; it is rather the taming of what is savage and base in our nature for what is higher and better. It is a release from imprisonment by our lusts and passions.

❖❖

God chose . . . to make a moral universe, but morality is impossible without freedom. Since He made us free to choose what is right, we are also free to choose the wrong. The eternal idea of Justice makes no one just, as the eternal Right makes no one righteous. In a certain sense, we are less free than freeable; we make ourselves free. Before truth and righteousness and freedom can become mature, they require training, discipline, trial, and the awful possibility of failing.

The whole purpose of education is to train minds to use freedom rightly. We do not take away the freedom of youths because they might abuse it. Hence, parents offer encouragement, reward, or praise to their children in order that they might choose the good rather than the evil. This is what God did at the very beginning. He did not give man the frightening responsibilities of freedom without at the same time offering him incentives to choose right rather than wrong. God would not force His happiness on anyone.

❖❖

It is pure nonsense to say that freedom consists in obedience to the will of any man, or that if a dictator supplies all the material needs of a people, therefore the people are free. It is false to indentify liberty with material abundance, for such freedom is the freedom of cows in clover, boys in jam factories, crows in cornfields, and the president of the Society of Militant Atheists in a sanctuary. Freedom does not consist in the abundance of material things that man possesses. If such is the essence of freedom, then there is no difference between a cat full of canaries and a Red leader full of caviar. Both are free because they are full. Such a view confuses liberty with comfort, willing with having. Liberty does not come from a full stomach, it comes from the spirit—that is, the right of a man to choose the good, whether his stomach be full or empty. Slaves who are treated well by their masters have all the material comforts, but they are not free to think themselves freemen. What good will material comforts do if a man cannot be free to deny that the State is omnipotent? What good are all the cinema tickets in the world if you have not the right to obey God according to the dictates of your conscience? Even if a state could be erected in which there would be no unemployment, no poverty, and an abundance of transportation to the country and playing fields, the citizens

❖❖❖

would still be unhappy, for with all that wealth they would still want to buy something which the State would not sell them because it did not have it on the market to sell; namely, the right to be free.

If we had to choose, it would be better to choose poverty rather than slavery, but since we are still freemen, we can choose the free way out.

❖❖❖❖❖❖❖❖❖❖❖❖❖❖❖❖❖❖❖❖❖❖❖❖

Patriotism is rapidly becoming a lost virtue; too many of our citizens think of freedom only as the right to make a speech; of tolerance only as indifference to right and wrong; of liberalism only as the surrender of tradition, constitutions, and the valuc of a person; and of democracy as only the catchword with which to involve American interests in international brigandage.

❖❖❖

THE YOUNG WORLD

THE   WORLD

Modern art, which is so expressive of the times, rarely paints a man such as one sees on the street. In one of the classic paintings of modern man, he has only one eye; the rest of him is made up of squares, cubes, cross lines, and meaningless figures all combining to indicate complexity, diversity, tension, multiplicity, and chaos. Every now and then a good thought may cross such a mind, but it has no roots. It is like magazines which editorially plead for a more disciplined youth and then on the other pages do everything, through pictures of excesses and merry carousing, to destroy it.

❖-❖

In those ages where maturity, sagacity, and achieve-
ment were respected, there was respect for tradition
and reverence for parents and elders. Youth would then
imitate the elders in their dress, just as little girls now-
adays put up their hair in knots and wear high heels,
and just as boys start shaving the "down" before it is
time. Today, maturity is no longer respected, and the
fashions are dictated by youth, so that old people dress
like young people. We sometimes see a pale copy of
the bloom of youth on the cheek of an octogenarian.
Short hair for women, at one time, was supposed to be
something very modern. . . . But short hair was almost
as common in the Grecian-Roman civilization. St. Paul
criticized the women of Corinth for wearing their hair
like men's. . . . Red fingernails were as common in the
luxury of Egyptian civilization as they are today, but
then there was no Dorothy Parker to say: "She looks
as if she had just gored an ox."

❖-❖

... are we suffering from a moral or a cultural degeneration? There is no doubt that it is a moral degeneration, but it involves more than youth. Therefore, it is a cultural decay. It oftens happens that an individual who is frustrated may look for some kind of escape in sexual promiscuity. So it is with society. When it runs up against a dead end, many aberrations—artistic, political, economic, and carnal—leave their sediment or scum on the surface of society.

Cultural decay reveals itself with society particularly in two areas: first in public life; second, family life.

In public life there is an evident want of integrity and honesty in such things as the primacy of the "fast buck," price-fixing, built-in obsolescence in mechanical things, the substitution of the novel and the new for what is already practical and useful.

In family life, too, youth sees the wedding ring cut in two. Thirteen million youths in the United States are "half orphans." Some see drunken fathers, others see neurotic mothers. The want of fidelity and love in the home makes them despair as much of loyalty in private matters as of honesty in public.

A... complaint of children is the disinterest of fathers and mothers in their sports, their games, their trifles, and their worries. Children do not like parents who talk *at* them and not *with* them. Every mother loves to hear the first "Da-Da" of the child, but later on she may fail to take an interest in the "housekeeping problem" the little girl may have with her dolls. The father whose child comes to him to fix a model plane may say, "Let me alone; I'm listening to television." Because parents have no time for what they consider the "trifles" of their children, later on they feel the penalty of this disinterest by the children's not confiding in them. Children are to be laughed with, but never laughed at. Making fun of a boy or a girl the first night out, ridiculing their harmless little affections, is to forget that encouragement is more important in life than a reprimand. The little girl who brings in dandelions as a token of affection for the mother should not be scolded for doing so; rather, the mother should find a vase for them and treat the dandelions with affection. The gifts that we bring to God are sometimes no more precious than those dandelions, and God accepts our gifts. Parents who complain, "Children today won't listen," are very often themselves parents who do not listen. Sometimes, of course, the questions of children become irksome. What parents call "silly questions" are very often those

48

❖❖

the parents do not know how to answer, such as that of the little girl who said, "Mother, how much am I worth to you?" The mother answered, "A million dollars." The little girl said, "Can you advance me a quarter?"

❖❖❖❖❖❖❖❖❖❖❖❖❖❖❖❖❖❖❖❖❖❖❖❖❖

In the order of nature, not many things are capable of being trained. Water, for example, is capable of assuming only three different forms: vapor, ice, and liquid. Crystals have their shapes rigorously determined by the law of nature. In the animal kingdom, it is very dubious whether fleas can be trained, though elephants and dogs can. No one ever says to a little pig, "What kind of a hog are you going to be when you grow up?" But one does ask a child, "What kind of man are you going to be?" Children are either trained by us toward a fixed goal and destiny, or trained in spite of us. The parents never have the alternative of deciding whether their child's mind will be full or empty. It cannot be kept empty; it will be filled with something. Passions, television, movies, streets, radio, comic books—all of these contrive against a perpetual vacancy in the mind of the child. Like a little octopus's, his arms are reaching out either for food or for poison.

❖❖

To those who say, "If I spank my child, my child won't love me," it may be retorted, "If you do not discipline your child, your child will never love you." A child can reach a point where he will have no respect for his parents. Suppose you tell a child, "Do not put your finger in that ink bottle." The child does stick his finger in the ink bottle. The mother wipes off the ink and says, "I told you not to stick your finger in that ink bottle. Now, don't do it again." The child thinks, "I will have to wait a minute; she's angry now. But I am going to do it anyway. All right! I guess enough time has passed; here goes." The child says, "I 'dood' it." The mother shrieks, "I told you not to do that." He waits thirty seconds longer this time, repeats the dunking act, and the mother pays no attention to him. From that time on, the mother has no more authority over the child. He is the master; she the servant. Mothers who are afraid to discipline think pain is more serious than wrong. When children grow up, they will not dislike their parents because they disciplined them when wrong, but because they never gave them a moral sense of right and wrong. Better the child's tears when young, than the parents' tears when the child is a man.

No child is ever born a skeptic or an agnostic. Agnostics and skeptics are made not by thinking, but rather by behavior, that is, bad behavior. A child cannot understand a lie. Everything the father tells him is absolutely true. He may even justify a statement by saying, "It is in a book," never suspecting that lies could be printed as well as told.

Suppose the parents completely neglect to train the child in the infinite eternal truth, which he already knows by instinct. The child will then begin to live in a small universe, and nothing is so small as a materialistic universe, or a purely humanistic world in which there are only struggling, weak men. If religious education is abandoned, as the child grows in age, the world in which he lives will become smaller and smaller until finally the only world that is left is his tiny little ego, in which he is imprisoned with his selfishness and ignorance—and he has to go to a psychiatrist to get him out.

The purpose of rules is not to restrain the child but to protect him against himself.

Picture an island in the center of the sea, with great high walls; inside of the walls children play and dance and sing. One day some men called false liberals come to the island and say to the children: "Who put up those walls? Can't you see that they are restraining your freedom and your liberty? Tear them down." The children obediently tear down the walls. Some time later, the false liberals come back to find all the children huddled together in the center of the island, afraid to play, afraid to sing, afraid to dance—afraid of falling into the sea.

False liberty goes to the extreme of favoring self-government before the child is ready for it. The child should move progressively toward autonomy. There is first the acceptance of the rule, then that interior adhesion to the rule which is the true sign of liberty.

A surplus of gushing affection for one's children is very often the result, not of true love, but of defective authority. It does not take a child long to discover that he can get from his parents anything that he wants. Such false kindness makes the child more rebellious because he knows, by experience, that the commands of his mother are never sustained by a firm will. He also knows that the more he revolts, the more his coddling mother will give away. A mother once said to her son: "I have had just about enough of you. Why don't you run away?" The little son said: "Listen, Mom, I am perfectly satisfied here. Why don't *you* run away?" A little brat who had been developed into one by self-will once prompted a stewardess on a plane to say: "How would you like to go outside and play?" The youth who gets everything he wants grows up to believe the world owes him a living. The socialism which holds that the state should supply all our needs is an extension of the coddling parent into the field of government.

The real basis of obedience in the family . . . is not the fear of punishment, as in religion it is not the fear of hell. Rather, it is based on the fact that one never wants to hurt anyone that one loves. As Our Blessed Lord said: "If you love Me, you will keep My commandments."

. . . respect for parental authority is never arbitrary, nor does it necessarily indicate an absence of a critical sense on the part of the children. The children have already made a judgment as to why their parents should be respected, namely, because of their goodness in providing them with their needs. Though the judgment is quite inarticulate and immature on the part of children, it is present, as shown by the fact that they will not take a strange person's word against the word of a parent. For most boys, "My daddy told me" is a final authority. Children arrive early at a point where they can make a judgment of their parents' credibility and a real adhesion of the will. A child certainly has more reason to trust a parent than most of us have to trust a radio commentator or an article in a magazine. The acceptance of parental authority is not blind and baseless; its foundation is love and confidence. Authoritarianism is based on force, and therefore is physical, but authority is founded on reverence and love, and therefore is moral.

Boys and girls separate into groups of their own sex. Boys, at a certain age, do not want to play with girls, and girls do not want to play with boys. This separation, or polarization, allows each to develop according to his or her sex; it is a time for physical and psychic differentiation. One of the greatest humiliations that can be given a boy at this stage of life is to be made to sit with girls; the same is true of a girl who is told to join the boys' group.

During this period of separation, the boys develop aggressiveness and aptitudes through their games, which prepare them for life. They develop chivalry, daring, strength, heroism, and mastery over nature; they tend to form groups as a prelude to community living later on in life.

The girls, on the contrary, develop sensitiveness, emotional qualities, refinement, ideals, and timidity in order that later on there may not be a too precocious revelation of the secret; there is also an introduction to the rhythm of the cosmos, and a reminder that they are the bearers of life and contain within themselves great mysterious and creative possibilities.

This polarity is essential for life; the negative and the positive poles of electricity are created, which later on make the sparks of true love possible.

✠✠✠

... if there is a too frequent intermingling at an early age, there is apt to be a marring of the psychic and physical development of each sex. Timidity may not be fostered in the woman, nor chivalry in the man, while a natural reserve may be wanting in both. Before the bow and the violin are to be put together to produce music, the bow must have its moment in which it is waxed and the violin its moment when the strings are tightened. A too early association is apt to produce effeminacy, unmanliness, softness, and weakness in boys, which spoil them for life. The girls, in their turn, if there is not this polarization, are apt to become impudent, boyish, and tough. Dating at this early age is likely to be bad for both body and soul development, for it leaves little chance for the unfolding of ideals. No young man wants in a woman the qualities he possesses; he wants in her the qualities he does not possess. He is looking for a complement and filling up of what he lacks. There can be no sparks when there are two positive charges of electricity. A normal boy is repulsed by a boyish woman, and an effeminate man does not attract a real woman. She wants a man and not a manikin. Since each must be given time to fulfill divinely appointed destiny, courtship and steady dates at this age are to be discouraged.

In a discussion concerning divorced or discordant parents, Bishop Sheen noted the following:

A child is much wiser than his elders suspect; he senses instinctively that his parents are representatives of God, and that he should come first in their love. If they betray his innate trust, if they violate his right to be brought up by his own parents, there is a predisposition to three types of delinquency.

a. Such a child will grow up not only cynical about women if his mother failed, or about men if his father failed, but cynical against God and religion. God, in his parents, failed his trust, so he will join future persecutors of religion.

b. Having seen the basic law of homelife flouted, the child grows up with a contempt for *all* law.

c. Influenced by a home where life's greatest loyalty has been insulted and abandoned, a child may even be affected in his love of country. The youth who has seen his mother leave his father finds it easier to throw over the heritage of America for allegiance to a foreign power. . . .

The principal cause of juvenile delinquency, in the final analysis, is delinquent parents in the home. Bad behavior is due less to outside environmental factors than to the temper and quality of the household in which the child lives. The great *D* of Delinquency has its roots in the three *D*'s which describe three types of parents: Doting, Drinking, and Divorced (or Discordant) parents.

There is a right way and a wrong way of choosing courses: the right way is to relate them to a pyramid; the wrong way is to consider them as bottles on a shelf. Courses should be related like stones in a pyramid. Not all subjects have equal value, or equal certitude, or equal applicability. Furthermore, some are essential for the understanding of others. The superior sciences illuminate the inferior sciences; for example, one cannot understand music or physics unless one understands mathematics. At the peak of the pyramid is philosophy, which is the science of all being, and which illuminates all other sciences.

The pyramid has been supplanted by the shelf theory of education: courses are arranged like bottles on a shelf. It does not make a great deal of difference what is in the bottles. Each bottle stands for a prescribed number of hours in the classroom; at the end of four years, if one can collect enough bottles, one brings them to the dean; the dean counts them, but he, too, ignores what is in them. If a sufficient number are presented, generally 120 bottles, the college, which has succeeded in pulling the wool over the student's eyes, celebrates its success by giving him a sheepskin.

This shelf theory of education has made it possible for colleges to offer courses which have no scholarly or scientific standing, such as courses in cosmetology, of the effect of the narrow-gauge railroad on Russian thought during the winter of 1897, or the growth of dialectical materialism in northeastern Missouri. Students are taught things that they do not need to know, and which they could find out for themselves in ten hours of reading.

A well-rounded education which will enable the student to deepen the mystery of wisdom through a lifetime must aim at giving an understanding of his four-fold relation: (1) to the universe; (2) to society; (3) to himself; (4) to God.

To understand the universe, the student must have basic courses in the sciences and mathematics. Unfortunately, because science is not subject to personal opinion, but requires a rigid training, there is a decline in scientific study.

. . . students today are not electing science; hence we see the queer phenomenon of education moving away from science, while life is moving toward it.

Teaching should cause a personal discovery by the pupil; otherwise, it becomes as food in the stomach which cannot be assimilated. St. Thomas says that a teacher must teach as an inventor invents. That is to say, he must be exercising his own intellectual activity during the lecture. If he is reading from notes alone, he is not teaching. He might just as well give the notes to the pupils and let them go home. The teacher must live intellectually while he is teaching; otherwise, the pupil will not live intellectually either. A professor who is not learning while he is teaching is not a real teacher.

━━

*Bishop Sheen, well aware of the tendency in America
to push her children into adulthood, explained why he
planned to defer administering the sacraments of con-
firmation to youngsters in his diocese until their gradu-
ation from high school:*

Bishops are now being asked to confirm eleven-year-
old tots who haven't yet reached the age of puberty. We
have forgotten there are three ages of youth—birth,
puberty, and maturity.

━━

The rat race and the meaninglessness of existence of some youths who live for kicks is founded on the false philosophy that life has only a present, a now, a moment. The past and the future have been knocked out. The past has been destroyed through rupture of all relatedness to parents, home, tradition, experience. Youth was meant to live very much like wheat in a field, not to be pulled up until it was ripe. Today youth, pulled up from the roots, lives its own present life without memory or tradition. One becomes like a pendulum outside of a clock, a carbon paper without an original, who calls all parents square. Where the past is not consciously repudiated, there is considerable unfamiliarity with it. Modern youth has little knowledge of two world wars, knows nothing of the Depression, and rather despises history as bunk. Convention is looked upon as a kind of restraint, a manacle, a straitjacket; the culture which formed them is rejected; hence the fondness for placards, protests, adding signature to signature against anything which permanently exists, whether it be religion, government, schools.

❧ LOVE OF GOD

Why . . . did God create a world? God created the world for something like the same reason that we find it hard to keep a secret! Good things are hard to keep. The rose is good, and tells its secret in perfume. The sun is good, and tells its secret in light and heat. Man is good, and tells the secret of his goodness in the language of thought. But God is Infinitely Good, and therefore Infinitely Loving. Why therefore could not He by a free impulsion of His Love let love overflow and bring new worlds into being? God could not keep, as it were, the secret of His Love, and the telling of it was Creation.

The rain cannot save itself if it is to bud the greenery; the sun cannot save itself if it is to light the world; the seed cannot save itself if it is to make the harvest; a mother cannot save herself if she is to save her child; a soldier cannot save himself if he is to save his country.

It was not weakness which made Christ hang on the Cross; it was obedience to the law of sacrifice, of love. For how could He save us if He ever saved Himself?

Your hands may be dirty with work, but your hearts are clean; you may not have the social columns on the occasion of a divorce, but your name is written in heaven as the husband of one wife or the wife of one husband, or the loyal and devoted friend to another aching heart.

You may keep dogs, but you keep them as companions of your children, not as substitutes for them; you may not have a college degree, but you know more than all the college professors scattered throughout the length and breadth of our land, who have not yet learned why they are here or where they are going.

You may be the tramp in the street, the old woman in the breadlines, the little child in the orphanage, but because you know God made you and act on that belief, you know more than *Einstein*—a thousand times more, for the man who knows how to get his head in the heavens is wiser than the scientist who knows only how to get the heavens into his head.

You know the secret of happiness, for since the world offered you so little, you looked for happiness not on the outside in material circumstances, but on the inside—for "the Kingdom of God is within you" (Luke 17:21).

The quest for God is essentially the search for the full account and meaning of life. If we but had the power to take our soul from our body, put it in a crucible, and distil out the meaning of that quest, what would we find it to be? If we could but make the inmost heart of all humanity speak out its inmost yearnings, what would we discover them to be? Would we not find that every heart and mind and soul in creation desires fundamentally three realities and only three realities— Life, Truth, and Love? In fact, so deep are these three realities, Being, Truth, and Love, that we can say the whole universe overflows with them. Of each thing in the universe it can be said that it is true, for it is related to a mind, and of each thing in the universe it can be said that it is love, for it is related to a will and a desire.

Nothing ever comes up to expectations. To expect perfect happiness in marriage or anything else in this life is to subject ourselves to disillusionment. Only perfect love can ever satisfy us, and perfect love is God. We all want infinite happiness. Those who do not concretely believe in God transfer the infinity to sex, or power, or wealth.

The major obstacle to pleasure is time. Because you are listening to me, you cannot listen to my show and another on a different channel. Whenever you enjoy yourself you are unconscious of the passing of time. Whenever you do not enjoy yourself you are very conscious of time. If you like this program you will say, "Time passed like anything"; if you do not enjoy it, you will say, "He has already talked for two hours."

Time also makes it impossible to make a ham sandwich of pleasures. Because we are in time, we cannot march with Napoleon or with Caesar; we cannot have tea with Francis Bacon and Aristotle; and we cannot converse simultaneously with Shakespeare and Virgil.

Therefore, the condition of lasting happiness is getting outside of time, where we will enjoy all the happiness of mind and soul and spirit at one and the same time. That is why timelessness, or eternity, is the condition of happiness.

When you buy an automobile, the manufacturer gives you a set of instructions. He tells you the pressure to which you ought to inflate your tires, the kind of oil you ought to use in the crankcase, and the proper fuel to put in the gas tank. He has nothing against you by giving you these instructions as God had nothing against you in giving you commandments. The manufacturer wants to be helpful; he is anxious that you get the maximum utility out of the car. And God is anxious that we get the maximum happiness out of life. Such is the purpose of His commandments.

We are free. We can do as we please. We *ought* to use gas in the tank, but if we please, we can put in Chanel Number 5. Now there is no doubt that it is nicer for our nostrils if we fill the tank with perfume rather than with gasoline, but the car simply will not run on Smell Number 5. In like manner, we were made to run on the fuel of God's love and commandments, and we simply will not run on anything else. We just bog down.

The Goodness of God means that God gives us what we *need* for our perfection, not what we *want* for our pleasure and sometimes for our destruction. As a sculptor, He sometimes applies the chisel to the marble of our imperfect selves and knocks off huge chunks of selfishness that His image may better stand revealed. Like a musician, whenever He finds the strings too loose on the violin of our personality, He tightens them even though it hurts, that we may better reveal our hidden harmonies.

As the Supreme Lover of our Soul, He does care how we act and think and speak. What father does not want to be proud of his son? If the father speaks with authority now and then to his son, it is not because he is a dictator, but because he wants him to be a worthy son. Not even progressive parents, who deny discipline and restraint, are indifferent to the progress of their children. So long as there is love, there is necessarily a desire for the perfecting of the beloved.

That is precisely the reason God's Goodness manifests itself to us. God really *loves* us and, because He loves us, He is not disinterested. He no more wants you to be unhappy than your own parents want you to be unhappy. God made you not for His happiness, but for yours, and to ask God to be satisfied with most of us as we really are, is to ask that God cease to love.

If you are a father, do you not like to receive a tiny little gift, such as a penny cigar, from your boy? Why do you value it more than a box of Corona Coronas from your insurance agent? If you are a mother, does not your heart find a greater joy in a handful of yellow dandelions from your little daughter, than in a bouquet of roses from a dinner guest?

Do these trivialities make you richer? Do you need them? Would you be imperfect without them? They are absolutely of no utility to you! Yet you love them. Why? Because your children are "worshiping" you; because they are acknowledging your love, your goodness, and by doing so they are perfecting themselves— that is, developing along the lines of love rather than hate, thankfulness rather than ingratitude, and service rather than disloyalty. They are becoming more perfect children and more happy children.

As you do not need dandelions and chocolate cigars, neither does God need your worship. If their giving is a sign of your worth in your children's eyes, then, are not prayer, adoration, and worship a sign of God's worth in our eyes? If you do not need your children's worship, why do you think God needs yours? If their worship is for *their* perfection, not yours, then may not your worship of Him be not for His perfection, but yours? Worship is your opportunity to express devotion, dependence, and love, and in doing that you make yourself happy.

❖❖❖❖❖❖❖❖❖❖❖❖❖❖❖❖❖❖❖❖

Our Lord reminded us that poverty and slavery no more entitle a man to the Kingdom of Heaven than do wealth and power, but that the rich man would enter heaven if he would be poor in spirit and the powerful masters would enter heaven if, following His example in the Upper Room, they would act as the servants to God. The carpenter's shop, therefore, is not a truism about the beauty of poverty and the holiness of slavery. It is a paradox about the richness of the poor in spirit, and the power of the masters who serve.

Socrates reformed the mind, Moses the law, and others altered codes, systems, and religions; but Our Lord did not alter a part of man, but the whole man from top to bottom, the inner man which is the motive power of all His works and deeds. He therefore makes no compromises, or concessions. He has a real contempt of a broad-mindedness which is synonymous with indifference.

. . . everyone else who ever lived told us how to reform the world; Our Lord told us how to reform ourselves. In a word He told us the world can be made better only by making ourselves better. Everyone else told us how to make the road smoother. Our Lord told us to turn straight around and take a new road, to renounce what seemed good, pick up what had been thrown away, worship that which was burned, learn that which seemed foolish, crucify not our enemies but our lower selves, purge our hearts, hate hatred, love executioners, transform our souls, and answer with the strong "No" of Christ to the foolish "Yes" of the world.

Our hungry modern world needs to meditate deeply on this oneness of the ideal with the very Person of Christ. Since the middle of the nineteenth century human hearts have been trying to live on system: on Humanitarianism, the Religion of Modernism, the Religion of Science, the Religion of Humanism, the Religion of Beauty, Freudianism, Theosophism, Spiritualism, Idealism—on a thousand and one mixtures of musty rationalism, moldy superstition, worm-eaten necromancy, soured philanthropy, simian symbolism, which have made mysterious mystics out of men only for a passing hour. But these frozen abstractions cannot satisfy a heart, for a heart cannot live on a system about Truth, or a theory about Love, or an hypothesis about Life. The human heart can live only on love. There is only one thing a human heart can love—and that is a Person. Make that Person one with the Way to be followed, one with the Truth to be known, one with the Life to be lived, and that Way, that Truth, and that Life will pull at a thousand heartstrings, drawing from them the sweet symphony of love.

Such is the Person of Our Blessed Lord Who alone, of all men, combines the Ideal and the Historical in His own Person. Because He is the Ideal there is the romance of love about His Person; because He is an historical Person there is the truth about that romance. Everyone else told a romance. Our Lord lived it.

✤✤✤✤✤✤✤✤✤✤✤✤✤✤✤✤✤✤✤✤✤✤✤✤✤

There is a general tendency in our day to frown upon those who believe that Our Blessed Lord is different from other religious leaders and reformers. It is even considered a work of intelligence to rank Him along with the founders of world religions. Hence it is not uncommon to hear one who prides himself on his broad-mindedness (which gives offense to no religion, and a defense of none) fling out a phrase in which Buddha, Confucius, Lao-tse, Socrates, and Christ are all mentioned in one and the same breath; as if Our Lord were just another religious teacher instead of religion itself. Simply because a few resemblances are found between Our Lord and a few religious teachers, it is assumed that they are all alike, that there is nothing Divine about Christ. This is just like saying that because most of the pictures in the Louvre are red, green, white, and blue, that they were all painted by the same artist.

✤✤✤

What is a priest? A priest is an intermediary or link between God and man. His mission is to do two things:
to bring God to man by the infusion of Divine Life; and
to bring man to God by redemption from sin. . . .
The first purpose of the Priesthood of Christ is to bring
God to man or divine life to human life. We have no
right to say there is no higher life than ours, any more
than the worm has a right to say there is no higher life
than its life. The very fact that man is never satisfied
with his mere earthly life is a proof of something beyond. Like a giant, imprisoned bird, his wings beat un-
easily against the gilded cage of space and time. He has
always sought to be more than he is: that is why he
has ideals; that is why he has hopes; that is why the
Roman emperors called themselves gods; that is why
man, when he forgets the true God, adores himself as
god.

Our Lord never sought to keep the poor satisfied with their poverty, nor the miserable satisfied with their misery, just because they were poor or because they were miserable. He glorified not the poor man, not the rich man, but the poor man who was not always poor; the poor man who once was rich; the poor man who by the law of detachment possessed everything because he desired nothing; the poor man who became poor, not by giving away his wealth, but by exchanging it for the incommensurable riches of heaven. And all this is only another way of saying, not "Blessed are the Rich" nor "Blessed are the Poor," but "Blessed are the Poor in Spirit."

Atheists encounter God in hatred, just as He is encountered in the lives of saints by love. . . .

. . . the hatred of God grows out of the realization that every human being owed his existence to Him, even at the same time that He is denied or a new false idol is set up, such as sex, money, or the ego. The soul's inferno is created by the rebellious mind and the perverted will of man. From this there comes torment—greater or less, depending on how much the pendulum is separated from the clock, the carbon from the original, the creature from the Creator.

Granted there is despair, man is the only creature who can experience it, and as Kierkegaard has so well said, "It takes eternity to make a man despair." Chickens never have any complexes, roosters no psychoses. No pigs have ever had an Oedipus complex and no hippopotamus an Electra complex. Even the best of Christians have a sense of "the absence of God," particularly when they sin. It is not the consciousness of breaking the law that disturbs their soul and gives them something of this uneasiness well described by modern poets; rather, it comes from having wounded Someone we love. This is why St. Paul repeatedly says, "Grieve not the Spirit"; the one who lives in the presence of God has an intimate sense of communion with Him, and anything wrong disturbs that communion. In fact, it creates a far greater uneasiness than any atheist could ever know because the Christian has had a greater love.

Picture two men marrying two old shrews. One of them had been married before to a beautiful young woman who had died. The other had been unmarried. Which of the two suffered more? Obviously the one who knew the better love. Thus there is a despair, and unhappiness, and uneasiness in the soul of a Christian as well as in the soul of an atheist, but the uneasiness in the soul of the Christian is greater, for he had the greater love.

Almighty God willed that just as any great painting should make us think of the artist, and every great monument should remind us of the architect who designed it, so, too, everything in this world should, in some way, remind us of Him. In other words, God made the world with a *Divine Sense of Humor*.

But what has this to do with a Divine Sense of Humor? Do we not say that a person has a sense of humor if he can "see through things," and do we not say that a person lacks a sense of humor if he cannot "see through things"? But God made the world according to such a plan that we were constantly to be "seeing through things" to Him, the Power, the Wisdom, the Beauty, and the source of all that is. In other words, the material was to be a revelation of the spiritual, the human the revelation of the divine, the fleeting and the passing the revelation of the Eternal. The universe, according to His original plan, was transparent, like a windowpane, and according to that plan a mountain was not just a mountain—a mountain was the revelation of the power of God; a sunset was not just a sunset—a sunset was the revelation of the beauty of God; a snowflake was not just a snowflake—a snowflake was the revelation of the purity of God. Everything told us something about God, for by the visible things of the world are the power and wisdom of the Invisible God made manifest. According to this plan, every man was a poet, for a poet is one who is endowed with this sense of the invisible, the power of *seeing God through things,* and such is the essence of humor.

MAN'S CONFLICTS
AND TRIALS

It is not always true that "nothing succeeds like success." The lust for success may make us work so hard that we beget failure. Businessmen low down on the totem pole of a big corporation may constantly send memos to the boss to attract his attention, with the result that the boss puts them down as a bore or a pest. Golfers who are determined to be successful as long-ball hitters try so hard that they spoil their rhythm and end up as dubs. A teacher who is resolved to be a success uses such big words and amasses such confused and unrelated blobs of knowledge that the pupils cannot understand him. I have found, after thirty years in universities, that the more books a professor brings into class, the less prepared he is. One of the greatest failures I ever knew as a teacher was one who used a cart to haul into the classroom his undigested but seeming knowledge. A speaker who yearns to be a success, cultivates poses, changes his voice, and affects humor, so destroys his personality in the end that no auditor believes him to be sincere. Elderly unmarried women who want to be married try so hard to succeed that they alienate men by forward approaches which remove from men all challenge and the joy of pursuit. Anxiety about success leads to failure.

There are three great passions in man which impel him to excesses in his desire for things that are good. These three are *lust,* which the modern world calls sex; *pride,* or egotism; and *avarice,* or greed, sometimes called security. Though they are not limited to any one generation, each has a tendency to be stronger in different periods of life. Flesh dominates youth; egotism and struggle for power are apt to determine a man's middle age. Avarice, or greed, is generally the sin of old age. The piling up of money becomes a kind of immortality; by making himself secure in this life, one unconsciously believes he is procuring security for himself eternally. Youth is apt to be a spender; old age is more inclined to be a hoarder.

. . . the best way to enjoy old age is to see in it a time for making up for the sins that went before, a living in hope for the joys that lie before one. But this takes Faith!

Jews, Protestants, and Catholics should unite against a common foe. It is not a unity of religion we plead for— that is impossible when purchased at the cost of the unity of truth—but a unity of religious people. . . . In a word, if anti-Christ has his fellow-travelers, then why should not God and his Divine Son? . . . we may not be able to meet in the same pew—would to God we did—but we can meet on our *knees.*

Men of goodwill must unite! The tragedy of our times is that the moral forces are disunited while the anti-moral forces are united. The State is becoming stronger, more centralized, as the spiritual forces are becoming more disparate. The Jews protest against the persecution of their people and sometimes ignore the persecution of the Christians. The Christians protest the persecution of their people and sometimes ignore the persecution of Jews. It should be elementary that where basic rights are concerned, men of goodwill should be united. No man has a right to protest against a persecution unless he condemns it irrespective of where he finds it, and irrespective of who is persecuted. The choosing between totalitarian barbarities has weakened the cause of democracy at the point where it should be strengthened. Someday I hope to see a parade in New York in which Jews will carry banners protesting the persecution of Christians, accompanied by Christians bearing banners protesting the persecution of Jews. Persecution is not exclusively anti-Semitic; persecution is not exclusively anti-Christian. Persecution is antihuman.

But there is still another kind of unity possible among men of goodwill, namely, a *unity for social purposes*. Outside of the faith, where we are divided, there is a common ground where cooperation between men of goodwill is necessary and possible, namely, the preservation of the moral law in political, economic, and international laws.

For example, we can be united for the defense of private property, for equality to all races, colors, and classes, for the betterment of the working classes, for freedom of conscience throughout the world, for a peace based on justice, and for the hundred and one other moral requisites of a social order, where men of goodwill can live short of a risk of martyrdom. It must, however, be understood that cooperation for the preservation of the moral basis of society must never be accepted as a substitute for religion.

This rests an obligation on all Christians to collaborate for the social good. It is easy for us to excuse ourselves from collaboration for social purposes on the grounds that politics are rotten, or that Communists hold important posts in government, or that capitalism is incurably selfish, and because of this to draw apart into a catacombal existence doing nothing except to chant the lamentations of Jeremiah.

❖❖❖

It is incumbent upon us Christians to maintain fellowship across lines of conflict if the moral order of the world is to survive.

❖❖❖❖❖❖❖❖❖❖❖❖❖❖❖❖❖❖❖❖❖

It is interesting that most of our relationships with other people are contacts, as one billiard ball contacts another billiard ball. We become like oranges in a box; we mingle with others externally, but do not commune with others in a common task: "News of the hour, on the hour" keeps us buried in the trivialities of external stimuli, lulling us into the belief that we are in contact with reality. The inner life is never given a moment to see ourselves as we really are.

❖❖❖

Why is it that something not at all funny on the street can be very funny in Church? If a bishop wears a miter cocked on the side of his head in Church, it is very amusing, but if you see a man on the street with his hat cocked to one side, you don't pay any attention to it. The crooked miter is funny because of the seriousness of Christ in Church. Pleasure is best when it comes as a kind of treat or surprise. People who are always bent on having a good time, never have a good time, because they have no contrast with what is a good time. If every day were the Fourth of July, nobody would enjoy firecrackers; and if every day were Christmas, no one would enjoy the feast.

Character is not made by a single act in the past. Character is made by what is called the *habitus*. *Habitus* in Latin is a virtue, and is made by repeated acts directed toward a certain end or purpose. If the end is bad, then you have an evil character. If the end is good, then you have a good character.

If I sat down to play at the piano it is possible, if you gave me a selection to play, I might hit a right note. Ed Wynn was once talking to someone who boasted that he knew operas very well. Ed Wynn struck one note on the piano and said, "If you know operas so well, from what opera does that note come?" So if you give me a selection to play, it is possible that I might hit one right note, but if a great artist like Rachmaninoff sat down to play, it is conceivable that he might hit a wrong note. But you would say Rachmaninoff could play and I couldn't. You would not be judging by the individual act. You would be judging by the *habitus*.

The world has one supreme test for character, and that is the possession of a virtue in a high and eminent degree. Many generals in our national history, for example, are ranked as great characters because of their valor, and many scientists are ranked as great characters because of their wisdom. Some are judged noble because of their love of peace, others because of their bravery in war; some because of their majesty, and others because of their gentleness; some because of their wisdom, others because of their simplicity.

But this is not the real way to judge character. The possession of one virtue in an eminent degree no more makes a man great than one wing makes a bird. Just as the eagle's power is measured by the distance from the extremity of one wing to the extremity of the other, so a man's character is to be judged not by the possession of one extreme virtue but by the expanse between that virtue and the opposite one which complements it. Christian character is nothing more nor less than the reconciling of opposite virtues. In other words, a really great character is not just a brave man, for if a man were brave without being tender, he might very easily become cruel. Tenderness is what might be called the other wing to bravery. In like manner, majesty alone does not make character, for majesty without gentleness might very soon degenerate into pride. Love for

Peace alone does not make character, for without the opposite virtue of courage, peacefulness could very easily slip into spineless cowardice. Wisdom without simplicity makes a man proud; simplicity without wisdom makes a man a simpleton. A real character therefore does not possess a virtue on a given point on the circumference without, at the same time, possessing the complementary virtue which is dramatically opposed to it; for what is character but the tension between opposites, the equilibrium between extremes. Thus St. Paul exhibits in his life the beautiful tension between zeal and gentleness; St. John the tension between overflowing love and uncompromising devotion to truth; and Moses the tension between firmness and meekness.

Just as every engine must have its flywheel, every springtime its harvest, every ocean its ebb and its tide, so every really great character must have its pendulum so delicately adjusted that it can swing between the extremes of the magnanimous and the humble, the lofty and the plain, without ever once being detached. Character, then, is the balanced tension between opposite virtues.

Our indifference to truth has resulted in our loss of the passion for truth. The result is that today there are very few ideals for which a man would die, or even suffer sacrifice. Our false broad-mindedness, if we only knew it, is born of our loss of faith and certitude. As we forget the purpose of life, we lose the dynamism to attain it; as we lose the basic certainties of life, we also lose the energy to strive for them. Because we have lost our passion for truth, justice, and righteousness, a lethargy and an apathy have so seized our civilization that we find it difficult to defend even the ordinary loyalties of life. We have no strong passion for great causes, no great hatred of evil, but only half-drawn swords and one-fisted battles; we have thrown away our maps of life and know not which way to turn. It is horrible to contemplate, but there is probably not enough love of truth in the world to start a crusade.

This loss of enthusiasm for the good has had the sorry consequences of permitting evil and irreligion to spread like a pestilence. Many men love truth less than others hate it. This is a grave danger for democracy. Hatred is rapidly becoming a stronger force than love, or truth or justice or righteousness.

... this war [World War II] has not been caused merely by evil dictators. It is too commonly assumed that our milk of international peace has curdled because a few wicked dictators poured vinegar into it. Hence, if we could rid the world of these evil men, we would return to a world of comparative prosperity. What a delusion! These dictators are not the creators of the world's evil, they are its *creatures*. They are only boils on the surface because there is bad blood beneath. It will do no good to lance the boils if we leave the source of the infection untouched. Have we forgotten that from 1914 to 1918 our cry was "Rid the world of the Kaiser and we will have peace"? Well, we got rid of the Kaiser, but we had no peace. On the contrary, we prepared for another war in the space of twenty-one years. Now we are shouting, "Rid the world of Hitler and we will have peace." We must rid the world of Hitler, but we will not have peace unless we supply those moral and spiritual forces the lack of which produced Hitler. There are a thousand Hitlers hidden under the barbarism of the present day. Peace does not follow the extermination of dictators because dictators are only the *effect* of wrong philosophies of life, they are not the *causes*. They come into environments already prepared for them, like certain forms of fungi come into wet wood. Nazism is the disease of culture in its most virulent form, and could not have come to power in Germany until the rest of the world admitted that we are all citizens of an apostate world, a world that has abandoned God. For this apostasy, we are all in part responsible, but none more than we Christians, who were meant to be the salt of the earth to prevent its corruption. No! It is not the bad dictators who made the world bad; it is bad thinking. It is, therefore, in the realm of ideas that we will have to restore the world!

There is a rhythm in fashions, as there is in politics; the swing is from one extreme to another. In politics what is revolutionary today may become custom tomorrow. Liberalism is supposed to be very advanced and progressive. But every form of liberalism is in reaction to the last form of liberalism. Liberalism in the eighteenth century was identified with laissez-faire capitalism; liberalism today is identified with everything that is anticapitalistic. Fashions, too, oscillate from one extreme to another; and what is thought to be modern is usually nothing but a reappearance of something ancient.

The reactionary wants things to remain as they are; the liberal wants change, though he is little concerned with its direction. . . .

The reactionary has rather correctly been defined as a man who has two feet and new shoes, but does not know how to walk; and a liberal as one who has both feet firmly planted in midair.

The reactionary believes that change in the present order is revolution; the liberal believes that change demands the repudiation of sacred and inviolable principles.

The reactionary says: "Johnny wears a green hat now, Johnny will wear a green hat in the summer, spring, autumn, and winter; when he is fourteen and when he is forty; he will wear it to breakfast, dinner, and supper." The liberal says: "No, styles and conditions have so changed, give Johnny a new head. . . ."

The reactionary, instead of working toward an ideal, stagnates; while the liberal, instead of working toward an ideal, changes the ideal and calls it progress. . . .

There are ultimately only two possible theories to account for the nature and the origin of man: one is that the life of man is a push from below; the other, that the life of man is a gift from above; the one is that man is wholly of the earth, earthly; the other, that he is partly of the heaven, heavenly. The second is the Christian conception: man is not a risen beast, he is rather a kind of fallen angel. His origin is hidden not in the slime and dust of prehistoric forests, but in the clear daylight of Paradise where he communed with God; his origin looks back not to cosmic forces, but to divine grace. On this conception man is supposed to act not like a beast because he came from one, but like God because he is made to His own image and likeness.

An animal cannot sin because it cannot rebel against its nature. He *must* follow it. We can sin because we merely *ought* to follow our nature. When you see a monkey acting crazily in a zoo, throwing banana peels at spectators, you never say: "Don't be a nut." When, however, you see a man acting unreasonably, you say: "Don't be a monkey." Man alone can be subhuman; he can sink to the level of a beast.

The peculiar thing about a man is that, though he may cease to act like a man, he never loses the imprint of human dignity. The Divine image with which he was stamped is never destroyed; it is merely defaced. Such is the essence of a man's tragedy. We did not evolve from the beast; we developed to the beast. We did not rise from the animal; we *fell* to the animal. That is why unless the soul is saved, nothing is saved. Evil in us presupposes what it defaces. As we never can be godless without God, so we never could be inhuman without being human.

The first deep-seated yearning in the human heart is the yearning for life. Of all our treasures it is that which we surrender last, and with the greatest reluctance. Titles, joys, and wealth, power, ambition, honor—all of these we will let go provided we can hold on to that precious, palpitating, vibrating thing called Life. The very instinct which impels a man to put out his hand when he walks in the dark proves that he is willing to sacrifice a part of his body rather than to endanger that which he holds most precious—his Life. Not even the sad fact of suicide disproves the reality of this yearning, for in every suicide there is an illusion and a sentiment. The illusion is that suicide is total destruction. The sentiment is the desire for repose or the will to shake off the worries of life. Suicide is not so much the desire that one wants to be annihilated, but rather that one wants to be at ease, which is just another way of saying one wants to have a different life.

The great scandal of western Christian civilization is that it is prosperous while the non-Christian civilizations, for the most part, are in want. Latin America, while belonging to western civilization, belongs to the economically poor group. The rough dividing line between the rich and the poor nations on the purely economic level is the Thirtieth Parallel. If one runs his finger around a globe of the earth, raising it above China, it will be found that almost all the education, health, welfare, and prosperity is found above that line, and almost all the hunger, want, and misery below it.

We can no longer live on crossword puzzles, television, deodorants. We simply cannot! We have had a thousand excuses. We have fiery urges; we say that we must satisfy them. Or we are used to our grand style of living; therefore, we cannot let our wealth go. Is not our Christian world in danger of being stuck with our electric can openers, our Cadillacs, our cocktails before dinner —not because they are bad in themselves, but because they are being used to fill up our emptied and peaceless lives instead of caring for those on the other side of the Thirtieth Parallel?

The affluent who are avaricious and make money the supreme quest of life generally reveal these psychological traits:

1. A passionate desire to accumulate;
2. A reluctance to give;
3. "The world owes me a living."

✥✥✥✥✥✥✥✥✥✥✥✥✥✥✥✥✥✥✥✥✥✥✥✥✥✥✥✥✥✥✥✥✥

The purpose of life is not pleasure. Rather, it is to attain to perfect life, all truth and undying ecstatic love—and this is the definition of God. In pursuing that goal we find happiness. Pleasure is not the purpose of anything; pleasure is a by-product resulting from doing something that is good. One of the best ways to get happiness and pleasure out of life is to ask ourselves, How can I please God? and Why am I not better? It is the pleasure-seekers who are bored, for all pleasures diminish with their repetition. . . .

✥✥✥✥✥✥✥✥✥✥✥✥✥✥✥✥✥✥✥✥✥✥✥✥✥✥✥✥✥✥✥✥✥

There are three rules of dealing with all those who come to us: 1) Kindness, 2) Kindness, 3) Kindness.

The basic cause of loneliness is the excessive desire to be loved, for this creates an atmosphere of lovelessness. The more we seek to be loved, the less we are loved. The less we are loved, the less lovable we become. And the less lovable we become, the less capable we become of loving anyone else. Like a bird caught in a net, we deepen our tragedy....

... the most immediate cure for loneliness is to show kindness to others. The search for happiness by turning one's back on humanity kills happiness. The slums, the city hospitals, the missions, the unloved, the ugly, the socially disinherited—all these are potential remedies for the darkest of souls.

A fear exists of being betrayed in human relationships, and this makes one more lonely because there cannot be a complete commitment to another. A strange man and woman met at a well. One said to the other, "I will not hurt you if you do not hurt me." To love is to make oneself vulnerable and softens one to a point of becoming a target to the "slings and arrows of outrageous fortune."

Another loneliness is to be found in young women whom men do not treat as persons but as functions or machines. Young men will plead love to them, but what they love is themselves and not the one whom they praise. The result is that young women find themselves labeled as replaceable parts in an IBM civilization. Drink the water, forget the glass.

Let the strong ask themselves: *How strong am I?* Am I master and captain of my soul, or am I driven about by every wind of passion? How long have I been able to stay on a diet? Or on the wagon? What New Year's resolution have I kept? Have I not resolved as a mother to be kinder to my children—and yet blast them even when I take aspirin for my nerves? Am I strong enough to cut down to one pack of cigarettes a day, as I wish I could? Can I resist a second or third cocktail when I know that it causes me to make everyone in the office uncomfortable? How strong am I in resisting lust or dishonesty?

How rich am I when I look at the poverty of my inner life? I may *have* something, but *am* I anything? . . . How wise am I? I may know all the Books of the Month, being proud of my college education, but have I ever discovered the meaning of life? Is there anything lovable in me at all? Am I not nasty and cranky? Do I not short-circuit every conversation with a fellow worker at the water cooler?

But I still love myself. I am good to myself. I give myself a good chair when I come into the room. I always order the best food, avoiding anything which does not flatter my palate. I avoid conversations which might embarrass me.

If then I can love myself, despite all of my weaknesses, failures, and faults, why can I not love my neighbor, despite all of his faults? If I am really not rich at all, except on the outside, but inwardly poor, then why can I not really love the poor, who are richer on the inside than I? Why cannot I love others, despite the way they are?

❖❖❖❖❖❖❖❖❖❖❖❖❖❖❖❖❖❖❖❖❖❖❖❖

Only two classes of minds ever discover Truth: those who know that they know nothing and those who know they do not know everything—never the man with one book; never the man who thinks that he knows.

❖❖

One wonders if there is not mere sympathy in smaller communities than in great cities. One can live in apartments and not know the next-door neighbor, but there is hardly a village in which one does not know the next-door neighbor. There is probably less borrowing in all the apartments of New York than there is in a village of five hundred. Not long ago, a picture magazine took photographs for one hour of people who passed by a wounded man on a subway stair. The magazine recounted in pictures the number who looked at the man and then went on their way without making a sympathetic inquiry. But the magazine itself forgot to state that the photographer was more interested in the click of his machine than he was in the tick of the heart of the wounded man.

True leisure is not interruption from work, a coffee break, a recess. It is not at all in the same line as work, but rather passes at right angles to it. It is not a pick-me-up for work. It is not something for "iron-poor blood." Leisure is the capacity to raise the heart and mind out of the workaday world, to get in touch with superhuman life-giving powers. It is a recognition that "every man has a hole in his head" into which, as William James has said, "saving influences pour."

There is nothing from which the modern mind is more anxious to escape than the depressing bogey of monotony. It hates the mere fact of repetition just as much as it loves the shock of the new. The hatred of monotony is the explanation for many of the distorted views of life and action.

. . . if one asks just why monotony is so distasteful to our age, one is met with this answer: Everything that is full of life loves change, for the characteristic of life is movement toward a new goal, and urges toward new pleasures. Being essentially directed to novelty, life can never rest in the tediousness of repetition.

This argument has never appealed to thinking men as thoroughly sound. I believe that just the contrary is true, and instead of saying that those who are full of life hate monotony, we should say that those who are full of life find a positive thrill in monotony. . . .

There have been statements made recently that the confessional can be supplanted by psychoanalysis. This, however, is not true. The confession cannot be supplanted by psychoanalysis. There is a twofold difference between psychoanalysis and confession: the first is in what is told, the second is the reason for telling it. Psychoanalysis is the communication of mind with mind; the confessional is the communication of conscience with conscience. In psychoanalysis there is merely a confession of ideas, and the confession of ideas costs nothing and never craves pardon. In fact, there may be boastfulness about the confession of ideas. There are half-baked intellectualists who would boast of being atheistic, or who would say, I am an unbeliever; I am an agnostic; I am a nihilist. It is very easy to hold ideas, even ideas that have terrible consequences, but confession is not the communication of ideas; it is the communication of wills, and that is what makes it difficult. The mind does not blush in confessing that it is an atheist, but the will does blush when it admits that it has done wrong because the will is under the domain of conscience. Even without an act, the sinner will blush sometimes at his own degraded intention, though no one in the world knows about it but himself. And the real healing of wounded hearts and wounded souls is not by the confession of wrong ideas but by the con-

fession of wrong intentions and sinful deeds, not by
telling of ideas but by the confession of sins, and that is
why psychoanalysis may always develop in the way of
pride, while confession will always develop in the way
of humility and pardon.

❖❖❖❖❖❖❖❖❖❖❖❖❖❖❖❖❖❖❖❖❖❖❖❖

Why must we always think of our subconscious as a
garbage pail instead of a dinner table? Why conceive
that the energy of electric power is to give us a shock
and not light and heat? Are there only snakes under-
ground, or do we also find gold? Does not the depths of
the soul shoot up oil and fountains of water, as well as
being the centers of earthquakes? The time has come
when psychiatrists must see the subconscious not just
as a mudhole where pigs love to wallow but also as a
runway where planes take off for a flight into the sky.
The subconscious may be a basement, but it is one
where we not only throw out refuse, but also keep our
groceries, our hobbies, and our playroom and our wine.

❖❖❖

A remark not to be taken too lightly is one to the effect that the modern world is taking itself too seriously. Whether there be only five senses or fifty-seven senses, one of the most precious of them all is the one the modern world is rapidly losing, namely, the sense of humor. There are many evidences to justify this statement that the world is losing its sense of humor. Note, first of all, the changed attitude toward laughter. It was not so long ago that laughter was as free as the air, and as spontaneous as a sneeze, being the natural product of human fellowship, and the joyous effervescence of friend meeting friend. Now it is put on a commercial basis, and the business of making people laugh has become one of the serious enterprises of our country; in fact, so serious has it become that we are now obliged to pay about two dollars for an evening of it in a theater.

One of the really great needs of our own day is silence. Modern life seems to thrive on a fondness for noise, and by noise I mean not only the staccato barbarism of jazz, or the bleating and moaning of a saxophone orchestra, but also, and principally, the excessive desire for that which distracts—love of amusements, constant goings and comings, excitements and thrills, and movement for the mere sake of movement. What is the reason for this fondness of noise? It is not due to any inherent love of that which is loud, for people generally prefer that which is soft and refined. Rather, the reason is to be found in the great desire on the part of human beings to do the impossible—namely, to escape from themselves. They do not like to be with themselves because they are not pleased with themselves; they do not like to be alone with their conscience because their conscience reproves and carries on an unbearable repartee. They do not like to be quiet. . . . They do not like to be silent because God's voice is like a whisper and it cannot be heard in the tumult of the city streets. These are some of the reasons why the modern world loves noise, and they are all resolvable to this: noise drowns God's voice and stupefies conscience.

❧ THE WIT OF BISHOP
FULTON J. SHEEN

There was once a little six-year-old girl who was very anxious to help The Society for the Propagation of The Faith. She put up a sign on her front lawn: *Lemonade —5c a glass*. Many customers came back three and four times and soon the lemonade was gone. Her mother finally asked her where she was getting all the lemonade. The little girl answered, "From the cocktail shaker you had in the icebox."

Education preserves the American heritage through the development of character. Character to some extent is a little different from education. In education you always take what is best in a pupil. For example, education would never take hold of me and teach me to be a singer. I was telling someone at dinner tonight that when I first instructed Grace Moore, she said after the first ten minutes, "You have a wonderful voice." I said, "If I do have a wonderful voice, why can't I sing?" She said, "Have you ever tried?" (What priest hasn't?) She then asked, "What is your favorite duet?" I said, " '*Anges Purs*' from Faust." She said, "Let's sing it."

Well, we sang it. It goes up about eight octaves each verse. She finally stopped and said, "You are right. You can't sing."

Ignorance is not identical with evil. Evil comes from the will and from bad choices. That is why the preservation of the American heritage requires a certain amount of discipline. Is education forgetting it? How little of memory work there is in modern education. . . . Memory has to be trained when we are young. It is a very good discipline. Spelling is a very good discipline. Then there are moral disciplines. There is nothing that develops character like a pat on the back, provided it is given often enough, hard enough, and—low enough!

In an address to both houses of the New York State Legislature:

"I'm not going to pray for you. There are certain things a man has to do for himself. He has to blow his own nose, make his own love, and say his own prayers."

❖❖

In response to an audience's prolonged applause as he approached the speaker's podium:

"Applause before a speaker begins his talk is an act of faith. Applause during the speech is an act of hope. Applause after he has concluded is an act of charity."

❖❖

Garry Moore once received a television award for his spontaneity, and he then turned around and paid tribute to "the four guys responsible for my spontaneity—my writers."

The next to receive an award was Bishop Sheen, who said, "I also want to pay tribute to my four writers—Matthew, Mark, Luke, and John!"

Two Irishmen, Murphy and Kelly, were bitter rivals. An angel was sent to pacify Murphy. "You are very bitter and cold and cruel toward Kelly; to cure you, the Good Lord has promised to give you one of anything in the world if you will only let Kelly have two of them."

"If I am head of one labor union," Murphy said, "does that mean Kelly will be head of two?"

The angel replied, "Yes."

"If I win the Irish Sweepstakes once, Kelly wins twice?"

"That's right."

"And if I have a brass band following me, Kelly has two?"

"Yes."

Murphy then said, "Angel, I'll take a glass eye."

An eternally feminine problem is always: "What will I wear?" It probably began the day after the initial rebellion, when Eve looked up at the leaves of the fig tree and said: "I wonder which one I will wear today?"

Some time ago we received a letter from a mother who named her baby Fulton. Fulton is now four years of age. One day the mother looked for him; she shouted and screamed but got no answer. Finally, the mother went to the attic and there she found the little boy dressed up, with coat, hat, and a suitcase in his hand.

She said, "Where are you going, Fulton?" He replied, "I am going to New York to see Bishop Sheen. I was named after him." The mother asked, "What have you got in the suitcase?" He said, "My little sister. She's going, too."

A little girl was always lying. She was given a St. Bernard dog, and this little girl went out and told all the neighbors that she had been given a lion. The mother called her and said, "I told you not to lie. You go upstairs and tell God you are sorry. Promise God you will not lie again."

She went upstairs and said her prayers and then came down. Her mother said, "Did you tell God you are sorry?"

The little girl said, "Yes, I did. And God said that sometimes He finds it hard to tell my dog from a lion, too."

A mother one day said to a schoolteacher, "I know Reginald has been throwing inkwells out of the window, and throwing spitballs at you, but under no consideration spank Reginald. It will give him a guilt complex. Just hit the boy in front of him, and it will frighten Reginald."

It is not true that rules given to a child will develop in him a guilt complex. There are indeed guilt complexes, but they are abnormal. Guilt is normal to one who has broken a law. One must always distinguish between an abnormal manifestation of guilt and guilt itself. For example, a person given to excessive washing of the hands is manifesting an abnormal sense of guilt, but this does not alter the fact that behind this particular complex there may be a very real reason for a sense of guilt. A denial of guilt is a denial of responsibility, and a denial of responsibility is a denial of freedom. Illustrating the attitude of those who insist on having rights but no duties, freedom but no responsibility, praise but no blame, is a cartoon in which a psychoanalyst is pictured telling a mother: "Yes, your boy is stubborn, cruel, perverted, a kleptomaniac, has criminal tendencies—but bad, no."

The other day I was in an elevator in a department store. I was shopping on the fifth floor, and I wanted to go to the sixth. I stepped into the elevator and several other passengers entered at the same time. Just as the elevator was about to start, the operator said, "Going up." Some woman rushed out madly saying, "I don't want to go up; I want to go down." Then turning to me (I do not know why she picked on me), she said, "I did not think I could go wrong following you." I said, "Madam, I only take people *up,* not down."

Some athletes are good students, but those who devote themselves to the training of the body generally are not conspicuous intellectually. I heard of a college that was planning to have three football teams: one for offense, the other for defense, and the third to attend classes!

The Soviet concept of peace reminds one of the man who cornered his friend and said, "You say you are a lover of peace, Casey; then why did you throw the brick at Murphy?" Casey said, "Because he was very peaceful after I threw it."

Two Americans visiting Switzerland were discussing Europe. One of the Americans rather cynically said that there was nothing beautiful in Europe: "Cathedrals are old and dusty; the castles are without bathrooms; the art is not beautiful, for the most part it is religious art, having none of the squares and circles that you find in our progressive American art; there is nothing beautiful in Europe." His compatriot, pointing to the Alps, said, "But don't you think Switzerland is beautiful?" His answer was, "Take away the scenery and what have you got left?"

The best definition of an adult that was ever given is that an adult is one who has stopped growing at both ends and has begun to grow in the middle.

Recently, on the subway, I got up and gave my seat to a lady who was holding on to a strap. She was rather surprised and said to me, "Why did you do that?" Seeing that she was incapable of understanding a spiritual reason, I said to her, "Madame, I tell you, ever since I was a little boy, I have had an infinite respect for a woman with a strap in her hand."

. . . a woman's nature cannot dissociate sex and love as readily as a man. Her nature is much more integrated, and her elements cohere more gradually. That is why a woman is slow to fall in love. She will not give herself until she completely possesses the personality or is ready to be possessed by the personality. This is the safeguard God has put into her to prevent her from making a fool of herself, like the little girl who recently bemoaned, "He broke off our engagement. He returned my frog."

Teen-agers believe that they are falling in love with a person, but actually they are falling in love with the experience of love. All is not sweetness and light; it is a moment of life when poetry is written; the prose will come later.

The boy begins to wash behind his ears, demands his first tuxedo, and comes to an appreciation of a necktie. The girl, on the other hand, discovers lipstick and high heels and falls in love with any singer who can run the gamut of notes of one octave. During this period of terrific emotionalism, teen-agers come to the conclusion that "parents do not understand"; "they are old-fashioned" and "behind the times." They insist that this is the first time in the history of mankind that there was ever a young boy or girl in love.

This stage of crystallization and divinization is often called "puppy love"; this is an adequate description, for it means that if anyone mistakes puppy love for real love, he will later on discover he is leading a dog's life.

Most child psychiatrists today are opposed to spanking. A child psychologist has been defined as one who would never strike a child—except in self-defense.

A woman in an audience heard a preacher go through the Commandments, and after each Commandment, as he gave them in order, she shouted out, "Amen! Amen!" When finally he came to the Commandment "Thou shalt not commit adultery," she said, "Now he is beginning to meddle."

Bishop Sheen related that once, shortly after his eleva-
tion to the rank of Bishop, he made the first of his many
appearances on television, and stopped for a cup of
coffee at the drugstore in the building where the studio
was located, with his red cape already in place. The
girl at the counter, obviously used to serving actors in
every kind of costume, took the red cape very much in
stride and asked blithely, "What's yours, Cock Robin?"

Colleges are not grocery stores where courses are displayed like canned goods, from which the student selects either because he likes the color of the label or because he likes the salesman who offers them. Stephen Leacock once met an American student during a summer vacation and asked him what he was going to take that fall. He said: "Turkish, music, and architecture." Leacock said: "Do you expect to be a choir master in a Turkish mosque?" The student said: "No, I'm taking these courses because they come at 9, 10, and 11 A.M."

There is a difference between a person who is *dependent* and a *dependee*. The *dependent* is one who has a claim on society for a just reason. The *dependee* is one who, though able to work and support himself, nevertheless claims, "I have a right to live, and the world owes me a living." There is a Yiddish word for one of this type—*schnorrer,* a beggar who does not appeal to the heart alone but uses a veiled threat: "You had better comply with my wishes or else." A story is told of a *schnorrer* who asked a friend for money in order to celebrate religious holidays because he was unable to support himself. A few days later, the one who gave him the money found the *schnorrer* in an expensive restaurant eating caviar. His friend said to him, "How very inconsiderate, when you need money badly, to spend it on something so luxurious." The *schnorrer* answered, "When I have no money, I can't cat caviar. When I have money, you tell me I shouldn't eat it. When do you suggest that I eat caviar?"

Bishop Sheen began one of his speeches with the following story:

This is the oldest story in the world about women. Therefore, like wine, treat it with respect. After the Fall in the Garden of Eden, Adam was out walking with his two boys, Cain and Abel. They passed by the wrecked ruins of the once beautiful Garden of Paradise, and Adam pulled the two boys to him and looked in and said, "Boys, that's where your mother ate us out of house and home."

❖❖❖

In 1953, Bishop Sheen spoke to a very large audience in Chicago. He opened his remarks with the following:
I'm sorry that some of you have to stand for this talk. I include those who are seated. . . . It reminds me of when I went up to Rochester some time ago to talk, and I went into a barber shop in the afternoon. The barber said, "Are you going to this lecture tonight?" I said, "Yes." He said, "Well, you'll probably have to stand."

I said, "You know, it's a peculiar thing, but every time I hear that man talk, I always have to stand!"

❖❖❖

In Chicago for an important speech several years ago, Bishop Sheen captivated his audience by recounting this anecdote.

A Judge Dunn was seated in court in New York—or rather, in Brooklyn—while a very, very stupid witness was being interrogated.

The attorney said, "Were you at the corner of Fourth and Elm the day of the accident?"

The witness said, "Who? Me?"

"Yes, you," said the attorney. "Did you notice whether or not the ambulance came to care for the wounded woman?"

"Who? Me?"

"Yes, you. Did you notice whether or not the woman was seriously injured?"

"Who? Me?"

By that time the prosecuting attorney was exasperated. He said, "Certainly—you. Why do you think you are here?"

The witness said, "I came here to see justice done."

Judge Dunn said, "Who? Me?"

Bishop Sheen enjoys telling his audiences about the time, several years ago, that he was scheduled to speak at Town Hall in Philadelphia. He had left his hotel early enough to walk about the city. After strolling about for a while, he realized he had lost his way. He noticed a group of boys playing in the street and approached them.

"I'm a stranger in your city and I seem to have lost my way. Can you please tell me the way to Town Hall?"

One boy volunteered, and instructed him on how to get there. Then he inquired, "What are you going to do there?"

Bishop Sheen replied, "I'm going to deliver a lecture."

"On what?" asked the boy.

Replied Bishop Sheen, "On how to get to heaven."

"To heaven?" exclaimed the youngster. "You don't even know how to get to Town Hall!"

Several years ago when Bishop Sheen registered at a hotel in Minneapolis, he filled out a card at the desk. After the word "Representing" he wrote: "Good Lord and Company."

Several years ago, a scout for the New York Giants, Jack Lavalle, bumped into an old friend, Bishop Fulton Sheen. This happened in Pennsylvania Station and Lavalle states: "He asked where I was going, and I told him, Pittsburgh, to scout the Steelers. This was the same time that evangelist Billy Graham was holding revival meetings in Pittsburgh and Bishop Sheen said, with a twinkle in his eye, "While you're down there, Jack, how about scouting Billy Graham for me?"

An atheist is a man who has no invisible means of support.

An astronomer once remarked to Bishop Sheen, "To an astronomer, man is nothing but an infinitesimal dot in an infinite universe."

"An interesting point of view," remarked Bishop Sheen. "But you seem to forget that your infinitesimal dot of a man is still the astronomer."

❖❖

If you copy anything out of one book, it is plagiarism. If you copy it out of two books, it is research. If you copy it out of six books, you are a professor!

❖❖

I once received a telephone call from Washington from a lady who asked, "Young man, do you accept criticisms of your sermons?" I replied, "Yes, most certainly, but not anonymous ones. Who is speaking?" She told me and then said, "I found the end of your last Sunday's sermon very common."

I replied, "I thought it was common myself." She then said, "This is no joking matter. I am very serious. It was positively vulgar."

"Well," I said, "I want to repeat for you the last paragraph. I want you to tell me what is vulgar in it."

I had been talking that particular Sunday on the Incarnation, and the last paragraph was this: "There are substitutes offered for the Incarnation, but all of them leave the heart cold. Now we are asked to prostrate ourselves before the cosmos and adore the universe. Man cannot love the cosmos; man cannot adore the universe; man never has, never will, and never can love anything he cannot get his arms around, and the cosmos is too big and too bulky. That is why the immense God became a babe—in order that we might encircle Him with our arms."

I then asked the woman, "Was that it?"

She replied, "Yes."

I said, "Madam, I was talking about two things, the

cosmos and our Blessed Lord. What are you thinking about?"

She retorted, "Do you mean to tell me, young man, that I can't love anyone unless I can get my arms around them?"

I answered, "Madam, that is not my problem; that's yours."

❖❖❖❖❖❖❖❖❖❖❖❖❖❖❖❖❖❖❖❖❖❖❖❖❖❖

Just as, in economics, there is a marginal utility or a point beyond which a raise in price is no longer possible, so in emotions pleasures can reach a point of fed-up-ness. You remember the story about the boy who ate so much ice cream that his grandmother said, "You see, your eyes were bigger than your stomach! You have too much ice cream."

"No," he said, "there isn't too much ice cream, there just isn't enough boy."

❖❖

I gave a commencement address in Philadelphia at Rosemont College. Each girl graduate came to the stage, walked over to the side and received her hood from Father Sparrow, a teacher of philosophy. She then came to the center of the stage and received her diploma from Bishop Lamb, then the Auxiliary Bishop of Philadelphia.

When I arose everybody was tense. I did not want to talk to an unrelaxed audience so I decided to make a remark that was not particularly facetious or humorous. I observed that it looked as if the commencement exercises of Rosemont College had been planned by the great lover of nature, Francis Assisi, for every girl had received her diploma from a Lamb and her hood from a Sparrow. It really was not funny but that evening a little boy was asked how he liked the commencement address. "I liked it," he said, "but I didn't think it a bit nice when he called St. Francis a sissy."

A little boy in Long Island was turning the dial at about the time my television program began. Apparently he had never seen it before, because when he tuned me in and saw me dressed as I am and looking like a kind of "holy show," he said, "Oh, Mama! Look! Superman!"

On my way up to Boston I was seated alongside an Episcopalian clergyman, who engaged me in a discussion concerning the validity of Anglican ordination. He contended that he had Divine powers, that he could forgive sins, that he could consecrate. It is not to the point of the story to tell you how we argued, except to say that we argued all the way from New York to Hartford. He got off at Hartford. There must have been something of the feminine in him because he wanted the last word. So did I. As if to assure himself of the final and last blow of the round, he turned to me as he was getting off the train and said, "Remember, now, Father Sheen, there isn't anything that you can do that I can't do." I just had time to say to him as he got off, "Oh, yes there is. I can kiss your wife, but you can't kiss mine!"

❖❖

In an architect's office some blueprints were lost, and
the secretary was told to find the blueprints. The architect himself, perhaps just to ease the few moments in
which she was looking for them, said, "Did you hear
Fulton Sheen on television last night?" She said, "No,
I never look at wrestling."

❖❖

An Irish woman was traveling between the north and south of Ireland and had concealed in her baggage a bottle of liquor. The customs official said to her, "What do you have in that bottle?" She said, "Lourdes water." The customs official said, "Let me take a look at it." On examining it, he found five stars on the outside of the bottle, and the inside smelled exactly like Hennessey's. He said, "Madam, this is not Lourdes water. This is whiskey." "Glory be to God," she said, "a miracle!"

Duffy had a circus in Ireland. Almost everybody that came to Duffy's circus did so in order to see his ferocious tiger. It was Duffy's hard luck to have the tiger die in the midst of the circus season. He confided his sorrow to his friend, Pat Rafferty, who suggested, "Skin the tiger, give me a few good bottles of Irish whiskey, and I'll get inside of the tiger's skin, and nobody would ever know the difference." Pat had the drinks, got into the tiger's skin, and climbed into the cage. Those who came to the circus agreed that never before had they seen such a wild and ferocious tiger as the tiger in Duffy's circus. But just at the moment when he was putting on his most ferocious act, Pat spied out of the corner of his eye a lion at the other end of the cage, and all of the enmity between the lion and the tiger seemed to flood in the lion's eyes as he moved toward Pat.

Pat crawled to the door and then finally stood up and began shrieking, "Let me out of here! Let me out!" At that moment the lion fell upon poor Pat, crushed him prone to the ground; and as he felt the warm breath of the lion on the back of his neck, he heard coming from inside the lion's mouth the sweet and welcome words, "It's all right, Pat. I'm from Cork, too."

I think we make a great mistake in thinking that people fight because they hate. Actually, men do not fight because they hate; they fight because they love. If a man did not love anything he would not fight for it. Hence, there are certain common things that every man will fight for, the honor of his mother, and the honor of his country. If, then, a man will fight only because he loves, it follows that the more deeply, the more intensely, and the more passionately a man loves, the more he will fight. The Irish love more than anyone else in the world. Hence, they fight more than anyone else in the world.

There is a story told of an American priest who hired a "jarvey" to drive him about the shores of Killarney. On descending from the carriage after the trip, the priest offered him what he considered a very good fee; whereupon the "jarvey" took off his coat, threw it over the horse's head, and said to the priest: "Father, I'd be ashamed to let the horse see you giving me this."

If "blarney" means exaggeration, then another "jarvey" of Killarney comes forward to serve as an example. Last summer some friends of mine inquired of a "jarvey" if the lakes of Killarney were deep. "Deep?" said he. "Six weeks ago a young Irishman dove into the Lakes of Killarney, and last week we got a postal card from Australia asking us to send him his clothes."

There was an Irish cop in Central Park. I am not going to mention his name because he is a mounted cop and he falls off his horse occasionally and then has great difficulty getting back on. On this particular day he fell off and he tried to get on and he could not, and so he finally began to pray, and he said, "My mother's name was Margaret. St. Margaret and St. Patrick, help me back on the horse," and he made a leap but he could not make it, and so he prayed again: "St. Margaret, St. Patrick, St. Bridget, St. Kevin, and St. Columkille, help me back on my horse." He jumped again, but with no more success. And the third time he prayed, "St. Margaret and St. Patrick and St. Bridget and St. Columkille and St. Kevin and St. Joseph and the Blessed Mother, and all ye Holy Virgins and confessors and saints of Heaven, help me back on my horse." He jumped over the horse's back and landed on the other side, and as he landed he said, "Glory be to God; why did you all have to push at once?"

❖❖❖

Baloney is the unvarnished lie laid on so thick you hate it. *Blarney* is flattery laid on so thin you love it.

❖❖❖

A couple who had been going together for over twenty-five years without a proposal finally came to a crisis when the woman said: "Don't you think that we ought to be getting married?" He answered: "Oh, heavens! At our age who would be having either of us?"

Cain went bad because Eve never read anything on child psychology.